Solar System Explorers

Uranus

Written by
Rebekah Banks

KidHaven
PUBLISHING

Published in 2026 by
KidHaven Publishing, an Imprint of
Greenhaven Publishing, LLC
2544 Clinton St., Buffalo, NY 14224

Written by: Rebekah Banks
Edited by: Noah Leatherland
Designed by: Amelia Harris

All facts, statistics, web addresses, and URLs in this book were verified as valid and accurate at time of writing. No responsibility for any changes to external websites or references can be accepted by either the author or publisher.

Cataloging-in-Publication Data
Names: Banks, Rebekah.
Title: Uranus / Rebekah Banks.
Description: Buffalo, NY : Kidhaven Publishing, 2026. | Series: Solar System Explorers | Includes glossary and index
Identifiers: ISBN 9781534549913 (pbk) | ISBN 9781534549920 (library bound) | ISBN 9781534549937 (ebook)
Subjects: LCSH: Uranus (Planet)—Juvenile Literature
Classification: LCC QB681 B36 2026 | DDC 523.47--dc25

Manufactured in the United States of America

CPSIA compliance information: Batch #CSKH26
For further information contact Greenhaven Publishing LLC at 1-844-317-7404.

Please visit our website, www.greenhavenpublishing.com.
For a free color catalog of all our high-quality books, call toll free 1-844-317-7404 or fax 1-844-317-7405.

Find us on

Image Credits

Images are courtesy of Shutterstock.com. With thanks to Getty Images, Thinkstock Photo and iStockphoto. Cover – Dotted Yeti, AspctStyle, andreysharonov, FotograFFF. Recurring Images – thomas eder, YummyBuum, Sabelskaya. 4–5 – 24K-Production, Vadim Sadovski. 6–7 – bilgeari, joshimerbin. 8–9 – NASA images, buradaki. 10–11 – AspctStyle. 12–13 – Vadim Sadovski. 14–15 – newelle, NASA images, Vadim Sadovski. 16–17 – NASA images, ManuMata. 18–19 – Vadim Sadovski, Gorodenkoff. 20–21 – buradaki. 22–23 – Amanda Carden.

Contents

Words that look like **this** can be found in the glossary on page 24.

Let's Explore!

The solar system is a big place. It contains all the planets that **orbit** the sun. Join us on our mission to explore each planet!

Our mission is to collect as much data as we can. Hop aboard our spaceship and join us on our adventure to the chilly ice giant called Uranus. You will not need sunglasses here, explorers!

Where Is Uranus?

Each planet orbits the sun at different distances. If they were lined up in order, they would look like this:

Uranus is very far away from the sun. There are almost 1.8 billion miles (2.9 billion km) between them.

Uranus orbits the sun between Saturn and Neptune. See if you can spot them as we fly past!

Round and Round

To measure a year, we need to look at how many days a planet takes to orbit the sun. It takes Uranus 30,687 days to make this journey. That is over 84 Earth years.

Every planet spins on an **axis** as it orbits the sun. One day is the amount of time it takes the planet to spin once. A day on Uranus takes 17 hours.

Most planets spin in the same direction. Venus and Uranus spin the **opposite** way.

Planet Profile

Here are some notes on Uranus from our database.

Temperature

Uranus is minus 325 degrees Fahrenheit (-200°C).

Size

- Around: 99,018 miles (159,354 km)
- Across: 31,763 miles (51,118 km)

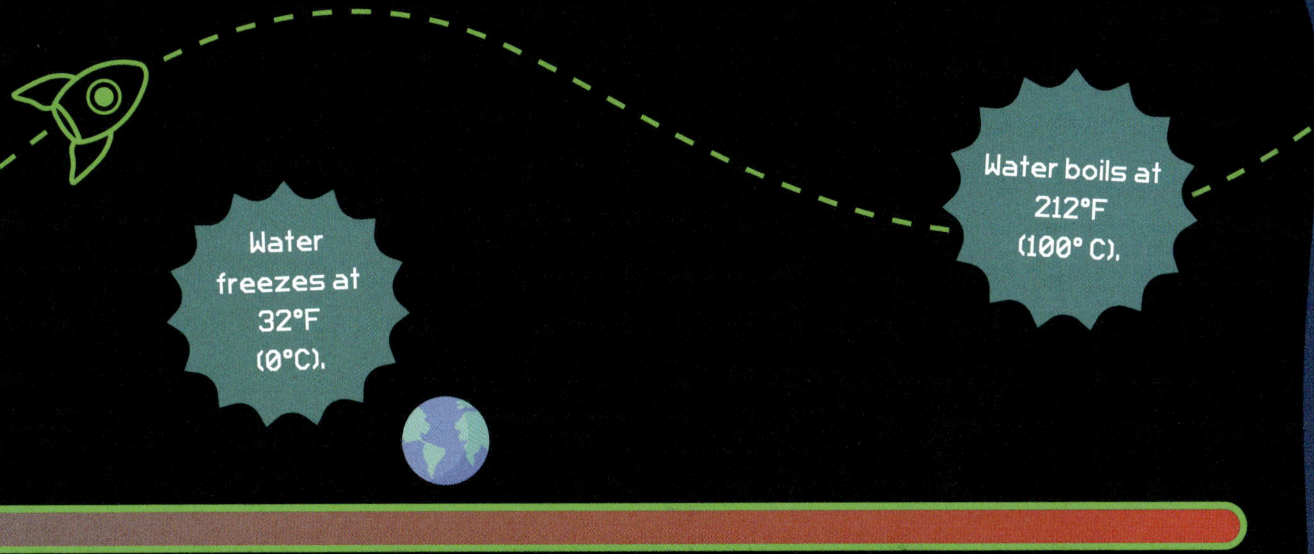

What Is Uranus Made Of?

Uranus is a type of planet called an ice giant. Uranus is mostly made up of a mix of different **liquids**. These liquids are water, ammonia, and methane.

Uranus is made up of different layers.

Atmosphere

Uranus's **atmosphere** is made of different **gases**, such as hydrogen and helium.

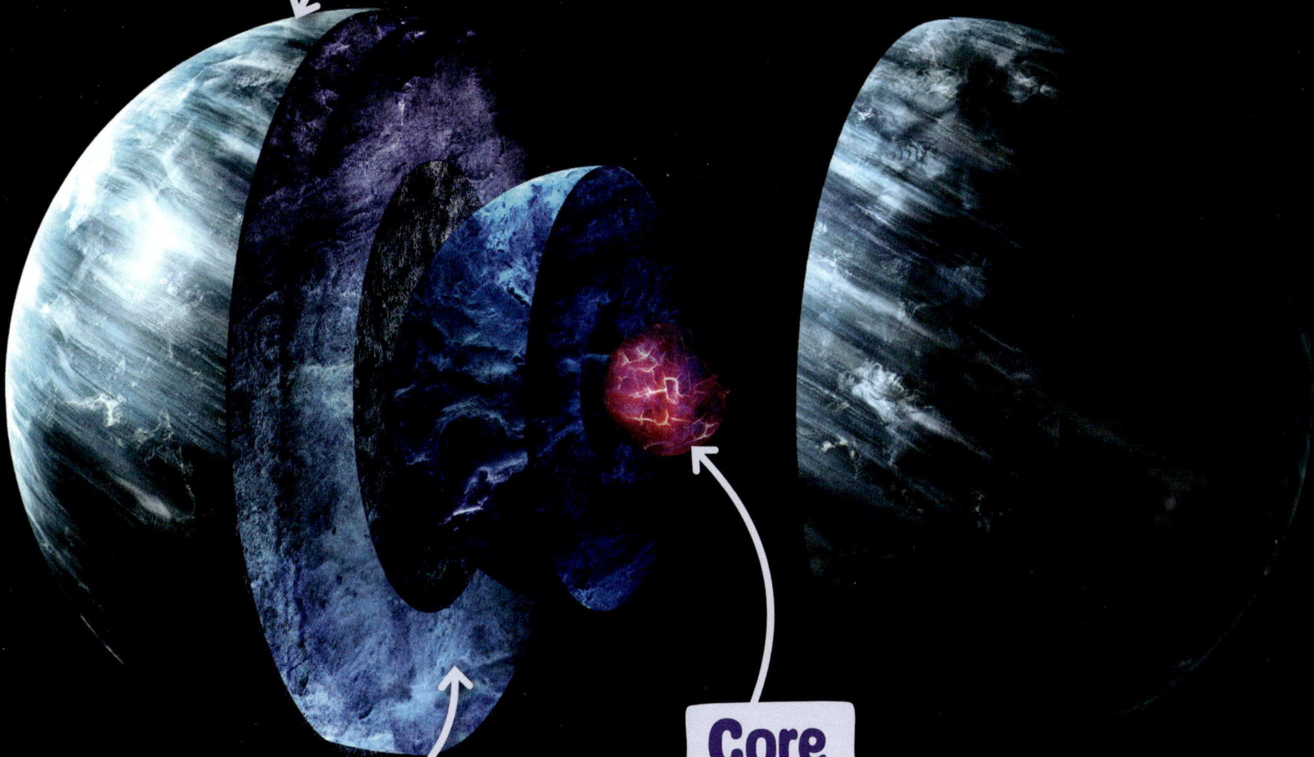

Icy Liquids

The liquid layer is made of water, ammonia, and methane.

Core

Uranus's center is made of a small, hot core of rock.

Watching the Weather

Earth's axis is slightly tipped to one side. This creates the different seasons and weather as Earth orbits the sun. Uranus's axis is tipped over much more. This makes Uranus's weather much stronger.

Uranus is covered by icy clouds and huge storms. Winds on Uranus blow at over 560 miles (900 km) per hour. The gases in the atmosphere make Uranus look blue.

Is There Life On Uranus?

Uranus is an icy planet with freezing temperatures. This planet has no **surface** and is full of swirling water and gas. No living thing would be able to live here.

Uranus may be too cold, but its moons might be able to support life. Scientists believe Uranus's moon, Titania, has warm oceans that could be home to living things. Can you imagine that? Fish in space!

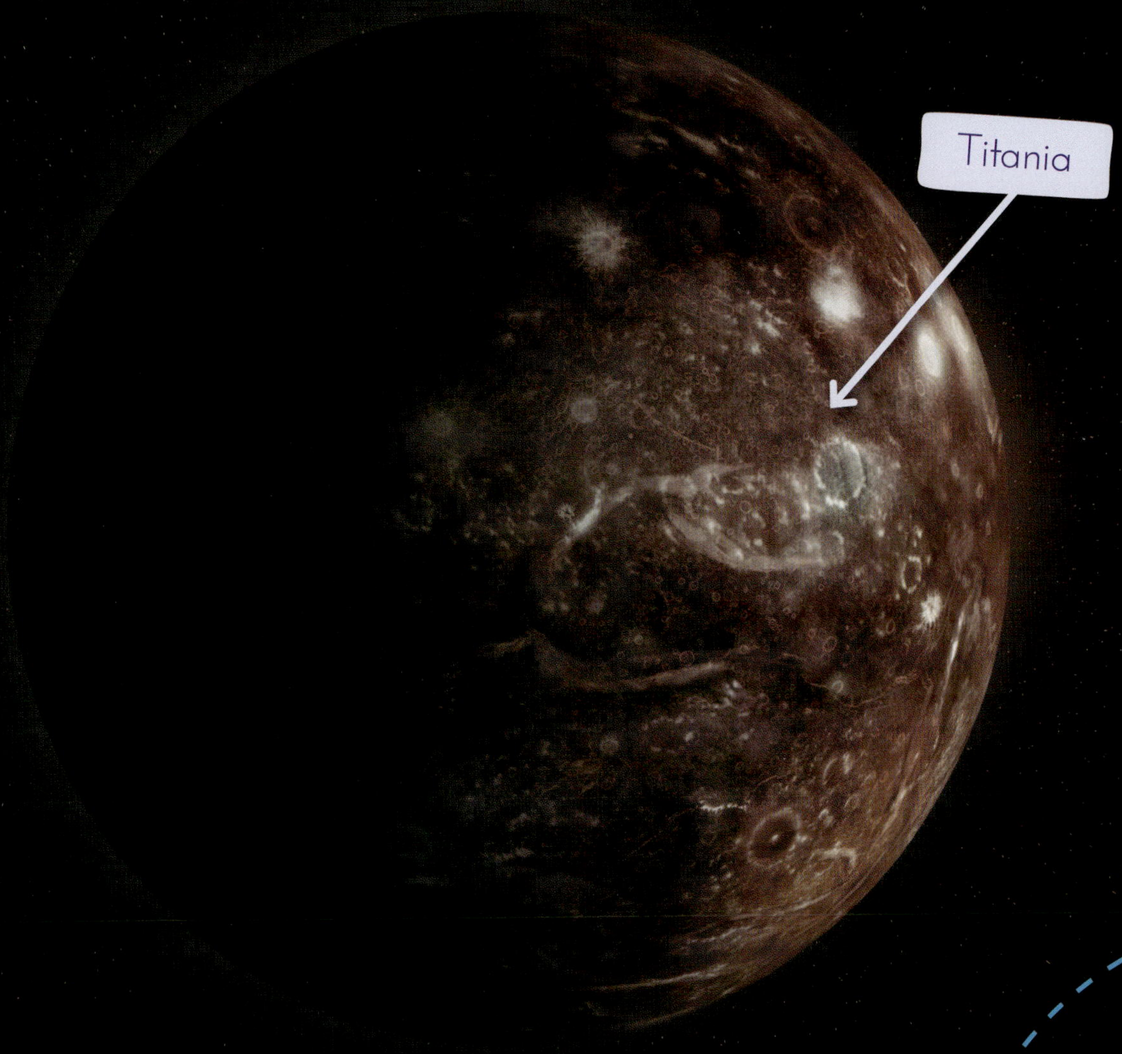

Spot the Satellites

Satellites are objects in space that orbit a planet. Some satellites are made by humans and sent into space to collect information. Moons are **natural** satellites that travel through space with a planet.

Uranus has 28 known moons. There are five large moons called Miranda, Ariel, Umbriel, Titania, and Oberon. The moons that are close to Uranus are made of water, ice, and rock.

Spinning Sideways

Uranus is the only planet in our solar system that is spinning on its side. It rolls like a barrel. Our database shows that Uranus may have crashed into another planet that pushed it over.

Uranus has 13 known rings. They are made of dust and rock that orbit the planet. As Uranus is sideways, the rings around it spin from top to bottom.

More to Explore

What a great adventure we had on Uranus! Our database is full of facts about this beautiful blue planet. What was your favorite thing about Uranus?

It is time to continue with the rest of our adventure. There are lots of planets left to explore. Let's find out what the rest of our mission has in store!

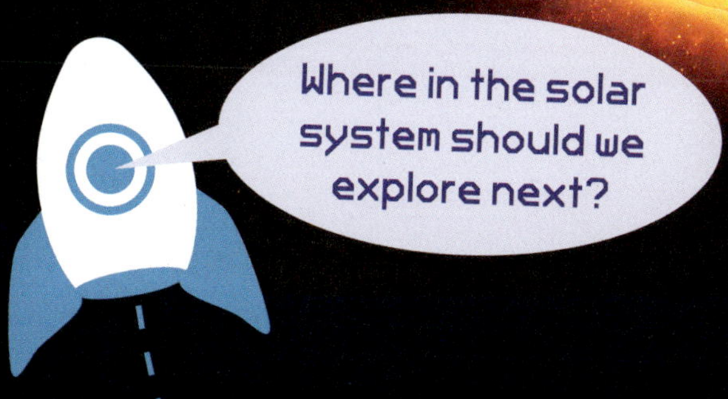

Glossary

atmosphere the mixture of gases that makes up the air and surrounds a planet

axis an imaginary line that something turns on

degrees measuring units used to explain how hot or cold something is

gases things that are like air, which spread out to fill any space available

liquids materials that flow, such as water

natural found in nature and not made by people

opposite completely different

orbit move around a star or planet in a curved path

surface the outside layer of something

Index